PLATE 1: *George Robert and Ruth Marie.*

PLATE 2: *Ruth Marie has a beautiful garden.*

PLATE 3: *George Robert and Ruth Marie take a trip to the desert to see the wildflowers.*

PLATE 4: *Ruth Marie and George Robert visit the airport.*

PLATE 5: *A trip to the fire station is always exciting!*

PLATE 6: *George Robert and Ruth Marie attend a fancy tea party.*

PLATE 7: *Ruth Marie and George Robert have been invited out to dinner.*

PLATE 8: *George Robert's baseball team is playing today.*

PLATE 9: *In the summer, George Robert and Ruth Marie like to go boating and fishing.*

PLATE 10: *Today, George Robert and Ruth Marie are bird watching.*

PLATE 11: *After a game of tennis, Ruth Marie and George Robert enjoy pink lemonade.*

PLATE 12: *Ruth Marie and George Robert enjoy bicycling on a brisk fall day.*

PLATE 13: *George Robert and Toby are waiting for Ruth Marie to decide which hat to wear.*

PLATE 14: *Ruth Marie is wearing a pretty green dress to her first dance.*

PLATE 15: *Tonight George Robert and Ruth Marie are attending an elegant ball.*

PLATE 16: *Ruth Marie and George Robert are going sledding on a snowy winter day.*